MIRRORS

Also by Robert Creeley

POETRY

The Charm
The Finger
Hello: A Journal
Later
Poems 1950–1965
The Collected Poems of Robert Creeley

PROSE

The Gold Diggers
The Island
Mabel: A Story
The Collected Prose of Robert Creeley

CRITICISM

A Sense of Measure

Robert Creeley

MIRRORS

In Mirrours, there is the like
Angle of Incidence, from the Object
to the Glasse, and from the Glasse
to the Eye.

—Francis Bacon

MARION BOYARS
LONDON · NEW YORK

First published in Great Britain in 1984 by
MARION BOYARS PUBLISHERS LTD.
18 Brewer Street, London W1R 4AS

Distributed in Australia and New Zealand by
Thomas C. Lothian Pty.
4–12 Tattersalls Lane, Melbourne, Victoria 3000

ACKNOWLEDGMENTS
Grateful acknowledgment is made to the editors and publishers of various publications in which some of the poems in this book first appeared: *The American Poetry Review, Black Mountain II Review, Conjunctions, Hard Press, Ink, The Poetry Miscellany, Rolling Stock, St. Mark's Poetry, Newsletter,* and *United Artists.*

'The Sound' first appeared in *The New Yorker.*

'Self Portrait', 'First Rain', 'Bresson's Movies', 'Beyond', 'Stone', 'Elements', 'If Happiness', 'Waiting', 'Still Dancers', 'Still Too Young', 'Some Echo', and 'Echo' originally appeared in a separate publication, *Echoes*, by Robert Creeley, published by Toothpaste Press in 1982.

'There', 'The Visit', 'Versions', 'Death', and 'Mother's Voice' originally appeared in the collection *Mother's Voice*, published by Am Here Books in 1981.

British Library Cataloguing in Publication Data

Creeley, Robert
Mirrors.
I. Title
811'.54 PS3505.R43

ISBN 0-7145-2823-4 paperback

Printed and bound in an original paperback edition by
Biddles Ltd, Guildford and King's Lynn

For Pen and Willy

CONTENTS

ONE

FIRST RAIN

These retroactive small
instances of feeling

reach out for a common
ground in the wet

first rain of a faded
winter. Along the grey

iced sidewalk revealed
piles of dogshit, papers,

bits of old clothing, are
the human pledges,

call them, "We are here and
have been all the time." I

walk quickly. The wind
drives the rain, drenching

my coat, pants, blurs
my glasses, as I pass.

MEMORY, 1930

There are continuities in memory, but
useless, dissimilar. My sister's

recollection of what happened won't
serve me. I sit, intent, fat,

the youngest of the suddenly
disjunct family, whose father is

being then driven in an ambulance
across the lawn, in the snow, to die.

THE EDGE

Long over whatever edge,
backward a false distance,
here and now, sentiment—

to begin again, forfeit
in whatever sense an end,
to give up thought of it—

hanging on to the weather's edge,
hope, a sufficiency, thinking
of love's accident, this

long way come with no purpose,
face again, changing,
these hands, feet, beyond me,

coming home, an intersection,
crossing of one and many,
having all, having nothing—

Feeling thought, heart, head
generalities, all abstract—
no place for me or mine—

I take the world and lose it,
miss it, misplace it,
put it back or try to, can't

find it, fool it, even feel it.
The snow from a high sky,
grey, floats down to me softly.

This must be the edge
of being before the thought of it
blurs it, can only try to recall it.

SONG

Love has no other friends
than those given it, as us,
in confusion of trust and dependence.

We want the world a wonder
and wait for it to become one
out of our simple bodies and minds.

No doubt one day it will
still all come true as people
do flock to it still until

I wonder where they'll all find room
to honor love in their own turn
before they must move on.

It's said the night comes
and ends all delusions and dreams,
in despite of our present sleeping.

But here I lie with you
and want for nothing more
than time in which to—

till love itself dies with me,
at last the end I thought to see
of everything that can be.

No! All vanity, all mind flies
but love remains, love, nor dies
even without me. Never dies.

THE VIEW

Roof pours upward,
crisscrossed with new
snow on cedar shingles
—grey-black and white—
blue over it, the
angle of looking through
window past the grape ivy
hanging from the top of it,
orange shaded light on,
place fixed by seeing
both to and from,
ignoring bricked window arch
across, just covered by
the light vertically striped
pinned to cross-rod curtain.

HUMAN SONG

What would a baby be
if we could see
him be, what would he be.

What stuff made of,
what to say to us,
that first moment.

From what has come.
Where come from—
new born babe.

What would he like,
would like us.
Would us like him.

Is he of pleasure, of pain,
of dumb indifference
or mistake made, made.

Is he alive or dead,
or unbegun, in between time
and us. Is he one of us.

Will he know us
when he's come,
will he love us.

Will we love him.
Oh tell us, tell us.
Will we love him.

TIME

for Willy

Out window roof's slope
of overlapped cedar shingles
drips at its edges, morning's still

overcast, grey, Sunday—
goddamn the god that will not
come to his people in their want,

serves as excuse for death—
these days, far away, blurred world
I had never believed enough.

For this wry, small, vulnerable
particular child, my son—
my dearest and only William—

I want a human world, a
chance. Is it my age
that fears, falters in some faith?

These ripples of sound, poor
useless prides of mind,
name the things, the feelings?

When I was young,
the freshness of a single
moment came to me

with all hope, all tangent wonder.
Now I am one, inexorably
in this body, in this time.

All generality? There is
no one here but words,
no thing but echoes.

Then by what imagined right
would one force another's life
to serve as one's own instance,

his significance be mine—
wanting to sing, come
only to this whining sickness . . .

Up from oneself physical
actual limit to lift
thinking to its intent

if such in world there is
now all truth to tell
this child is all it is

or ever was. The place of
time oneself in the net
hanging by hands will

finally lose their hold,
fall. Die. Let this son
live, let him live.

SELF-PORTRAIT

He wants to be
a brutal old man,
an aggressive old man,
as dull, as brutal
as the emptiness around him,

He doesn't want compromise,
nor to be ever nice
to anyone. Just mean,
and final in his brutal,
his total, rejection of it all.

He tried the sweet,
the gentle, the "oh,
let's hold hands together"
and it was awful,
dull, brutally inconsequential.

Now he'll stand on
his own dwindling legs.
His arms, his skin,
shrink daily. And
he loves, but hates equally.

GREETING CARD

for Pen

Expect the unexpected
and have a happy day . . .

Know love's surety
either in you or me.

Believe you are always
all that human is

in loyalty, in generosity,
in wise, good-natured clarity.

No one more than you
would be love's truth—

nor less
deserve ever unhappiness.

Therefore wonder's delight
will make the way.

Expect the unexpected
and have a happy day . . .

PROSPECT

Green's the predominant color here,
but in tones so various, and muted

by the flatness of sky and water,
the oak trunks, the undershade back of the lawns,

it seems a subtle echo of itself.
It is the color of life itself,

it used to be. Not blood red,
or sun yellow—but this green,

echoing hills, echoing meadows,
childhood summer's blowsiness, a youngness

one remembers hopefully forever.
It is thoughtful, provokes here

quiet reflections, settles the self
down to waiting now apart

from time, which is done,
this green space, faintly painful.

THE SOUND

Early mornings, in the light still
faint making stones, herons, marsh
grass all but indistinguishable in the muck,

one looks to the far side, of the sound, the sand
side with low growing brush and
reeds, to the long horizontal of land's edge,

where the sea is, on that
other side, that outside, place of
imagined real openness, restless, eternal ocean.

RETROSPECT

Thanks for
what will be
the memory
if it is.

ONE WORLD

Tonight possibly they'll
invite us down to the barricades
finally sans some tacit
racism or question of our authenticity.

No one will be ashamed he
has to face the prospect
of being blown up alone in
the privacy of his own home.

One can be looted, burned,
bombed, etc., in company,
a Second World War sequel for real,
altogether, now and forever.

MONEY

Stand up, heart, and take it.
Boat tugs at mooring.
Just a little later, a little later.

More you wanted, more you got.
The shock of recognition, like they say,
better than digitalis.

You want that sailboat sailing by?
Reach out and take it
if you can, if you must.

You talk a lot to yourself
about what you don't want
these days, adding up figures, costs.

Here in the rented house on the water
for the proverbial two months,
it's still not enough.

YOU

You will remember little of yourself
as you used to be. One expects this

familiar human convenience. I want
a more abrupt person, more explicit.

Nothing you did was lost, it was
real as you were, and are. But

this present collection of *myselves*
I cannot distinguish as other than

a collection. You talk to yourself
and you get the answers expected.

But oneself is real. There is, presumably,
all that is here to prove it.

MOTHER'S VOICE

In these few years
since her death I hear
mother's voice say
under my own, I won't

want any more of that.
My cheekbones resonate
with her emphasis. Nothing
of not wanting only

but the distance there from
common fact of others
frightens me. I look out
at all this demanding world

and try to put it quietly back,
from me, say, thank you,
I've already had some
though I haven't

and would like to
but I've said no, she has,
it's not my own voice anymore.
It's higher as hers was

and accommodates too simply
its frustrations when
I at least think I want more
and must have it.

DREAMS

I was supposed to wake
but didn't, slept
seeing the separate
heads and faces,

the arms, the legs,
the parts of a person
specific. As always
one was taken

to the end, the place
where the horror dawns
and one has killed
or been killed.

Then to wake up would be
no help in time.
The grey light breaks into
dawn. The day begins.

OUTSIDE

The light now meets
with the shuddering branch.
What I see
distorts the image.

This is an age
of slow determinations,
goes up the stairs
with dulled will.

Who would accept death
as an end
thinks he can
do what he wants to.

THERE

With all I know
remembering a page
clear to my eye
and in my mind

a single thing
of such size
it can find
no other place—

Written word
once so clear
blurred content
now loses detail.

THE VISIT

No resolution,
understanding
when she comes
abrupt, final

anger, rage
at the painful
displacement,
the brutal use

of rational love,
the meagerness
of the intentional
offering.

VERSIONS

after Hardy

Why would she come to him,
come to him,
in such disguise

to look again at him—
look again—
with vacant eyes—

and why the pain still,
the pain—
still useless to them—

as if to begin again—
again begin—
what had never been?

•

Why be
persistently
hurtful—
no truth
to tell
or wish to?
Why?

•

The weather's still grey
and the clouds gather
where they once walked
out together,

greeted the world with
a faint happiness,
watched it die
in the same place.

DEATH

Once started nothing stops
but for moment
breath's caught time
stays patient.

THERE IS WATER

There is water
at road's end
like a shimmer,
a golden opening,

if sun's right
over trees
where the land
runs down

some hill
seeming to fall
to a farther reach
of earth but

no woods left
in the surrounding
wet air. Only the heavy
booming surf.

AGE

He is thinking of everyone
he ever knew
in no order, lets
them come or go

as they will. He wonders
if he'll see them again,
if they'll remember him,
what they'll do.

There's no surprise now,
not the unexpected
as it had been. He's agreed
to being more settled.

Yet, like they say, as he
gets older, he knows
he won't expect it, not
the aches and pains.

He thinks he'll hate it
and when he does die
at last, he supposes
he still won't know it.

BOX

Say it,
you're afraid

but of what
you can't locate.

You love yet
distracted fear

the body's change,
yourself inside it.

TWO

OH LOVE

My love is a boat
floating
on the weather, the water.

She is a stone
at the bottom of the ocean.
She is the wind in the trees.

I hold her
in my hand
and cannot lift her,

can do nothing
without her. Oh love,
like nothing else on earth!

WIND LIFTS

Wind lifts lightly
the leaves, a flower,
a black bird

hops up to the bowl
to drink. The sun
brightens the leaves, back

of them darker branches,
tree's trunk. Night is still
far from us.

THE MOVIE RUN BACKWARD

The words will one day come
back to you, birds returning,
the movie run backward.

Nothing so strange in its talk,
just words. The people
who wrote them are the dead ones.

This here paper talks like anything
but is only one thing,
"birds returning."

You can "run the movie
backward" but "the movie run
backward." The movie run backward.

BRESSON'S MOVIES

A movie of Robert
Bresson's showed a yacht,
at evening on the Seine,
all its lights on, watched

by two young, seemingly
poor people, on a bridge adjacent,
the classic boy and girl
of the story, any one

one cares to tell. So
years pass, of course, but
I identified with the young,
embittered Frenchman,

knew his almost complacent
anguish and the distance
he felt from his girl.
Yet another film

of Bresson's has the
aging Lancelot with his
awkward armor standing
in a woods, of small trees,

dazed, bleeding, both he
and his horse are,
trying to get back to
the castle, itself of

no great size. It
moved me, that
life was after all
like that. You are

in love. You stand
in the woods, with
a horse, bleeding.
The story is true.

AMBITION

Couldn't guess it,
couldn't be it—

wasn't ever
there then. Won't

come back, don't
want it.

FORT COLLINS REMEMBERED

To be backed
down the road
by long view

of life's imponderable
echo of time spent
car's blown motor

town on edge of
wherever fifty
bucks you're lucky.

BEYOND

Whether in the world below or above,
one was to come to it,
rejected, accepted, in some

specific balance. There was to be
a reckoning, a judgment
unavoidable, and one would know

at last the fact of a life lived,
objectively, divinely, as it were,
acknowledged in whatever faith.

So that looking now for where
"an ampler aether clothes the meads with roseate
  light,"
or simply the "pallid plains of asphodel,"

the vagueness, the question, goes in,
discovers only emptiness—as if
the place itself had been erased,

was only forever an idea and
could never be found nor had it been.
And there was nothing ever beyond.

STONE

Be as careful, as rational,
as you will but know
nothing of such kind is true

more than fits the skin
and so covers what's within
with another soft covering

that can leave the bones alone,
that can be as it will alone,
and stays as quiet, as stable, as stone.

ELEMENTS

Sky cries down
and water looks up.

Air feels everywhere
sudden bumps, vague emptiness.

Fire burns. Earth is left
a waste, inhuman.

STILL TOO YOUNG

I was talking to older
man on the phone

who's saying something
and something are five

when I think it's four,
and all I'd hoped for

is going up in abstract smoke,
and this call is from California

and selling a house,
in fact, two houses,

is losing me money more
than I can afford to,

and I thought I was winning
but I'm losing again

but I'm too old to do it again
and still too young to die.

SAD ADVICE

If it isn't fun, don't do it.
You'll have to do enough that isn't.

Such is life, like they say,
no one gets away without paying

and since you don't get to keep it
anyhow, who needs it.

TWO KIDS

Two kids, small
black sculpture. In
trepidation she turns

to him who bends
forward to, as they say,
assist her. It is,

the proposal is,
her fear provokes her,
fear of a frog

crouching at the far
end of this banal, small,
heavy hunk of metal

must have cost a
pretty penny so
to arouse in mind's

back recesses
a comfortable sense
of incest? Or else

the glass table top on which it sits
so isolates this meager action
—or else the vegetation,

the fern stalks, beside them
hang over, making privacy
a seeming thought

of these two who,
as Keats said, will never move
nor will any of it

beyond the moment,
the small minutes of some hour,
like waiting in a dentist's office.

WISHES

for John and Debora Daley

Lunch with its divers
orders of sliced
chicken going by on

the lazy susan with
the cucumber, the goat cheese,
the remnants of the rice

salad left from last night.
All in a whirl the participants
and their very young

children eat, and
drink, and watch for
the familial move will

betoken home ground
in the heat of sultry summer
through the wall to wall

glass and beyond to the oaks,
the exhilarated grass, the
fall off to the marshy

waters, the long legged white
birds spearing fish.
Are we not well met

here, factually nowhere
ever known to us before,
and will we not forever

now remember this? One wonders,
and hopes, loves, conjectures
as to the lives of others,

all others, from other worlds
still here and always
everywhere about us, none

to be left out. No
memory, no thought,
less. Nothing forgot.

ECHOES

Step through the mirror,
faint with the old desire.

Want it again,
never mind who's the friend.

Say yes to the wasted
empty places. The guesses

were as good as any.
No mistakes.

SUMMER

The last waltz
pale days
jesus freaks
empty hours

of sitting around
thinking and drinking
being home
in a rented house

for the summer only
while the folks are away
and we get to use it
so long as we pay.

IF

If your hair was brown
and isn't now,
if your hands were strong
and now you falter,

if your eyes were sharp
and now they blur,
your step confident
and now it's careful—

you've had the world,
such as you got.
There's nothing more,
there never was.

IF HAPPINESS

If happiness were
simple joy, bird,

beast or flower
were the so-called world

here everywhere
about us,

then love were as true
as air, as water—

as sky's light, ground's
solidness, rock's hardness,

for us, in us,
of us.

WAITING

Were you counting the days
from now till then

to what end,
what to discover,

which wasn't known
over and over?

STILL DANCERS

Set the theme
with a cadence
of love's old
sweet song—

No harm in
the emotional
nor in remembering all
you can or want to.

Let the faint, faded music
pour forth its wonder
and bewitch whom it will,
still dancers under the moon.

THE FACES

The faces with anticipated youth
look out from the current
identifications, judge or salesman,
the neighbor, the man who killed,

mattering only as the sliding world
they betoken, the time it never
mattered to accumulate, the fact that
nothing mattered but for what one

could make of it, some passing,
oblique pleasure, a pain immense
in its intensity, a sly but
insistent yearning to outwit it

all, be different, move far, far
away, avoid forever the girl
next door, whose cracked, wrinkled
smile will still persist, still know you.

TO SAY IT

Just now at five
the light's caught the north
side of the trees next
door, the extensive

lawn to the sea's
edge where the marsh grass
seems a yellowish
green haze in late

afternoon. Above, the clouds
move over, storm's edge
passes in bunches of fluffy
soft dark-centered blobs,

all going or gone
as the wind freshens
from the land, blowing out
to sea. Now by the edge

of the window glass at the level
of the floor the grass
has become particularized
in the late light, each

edge of grass stalk
a tenacious fact of being there,
not words only, but only words,
only these words, to say it.

If, as in a bottle, the message
has been placed, if air, water
and earth try to say so with
human agency, no matter the imperfect,

useless gesture, all that is lost,
or mistaken, the arrogance
of trying to, the light comes again,
comes here, after brief darkness is still here.

SOME ECHO

The ground seems almost stolid
alongside the restless water,
surface now rippled by wind
echoed by the myriad tree branches—

and thought is a patient security then,
a thing in mind at best or else
some echo of physical world
it is but can know nothing of.

THREE

SUCH FLOWERS

Such flowers can bloom
blurred harsh

winter days
in house so

quietly empty.
Delight in leaves

uplifting to
cold neon or gangling

out toward faint
grey window light.

BUFFALO EVENING

Steady, the evening fades
up the street into sunset
over the lake. Winter sits

quiet here, snow piled
by the road, the walks stamped
down or shoveled. The kids

in the time before dinner are
playing, sliding on the old ice.
The dogs are out, walking,

and it's soon inside again,
with the light gone. Time
to eat, to think of it all.

WINTER

Snow lifts it
by slowing

the movement expected,
makes walking

slower, harder,
makes face ache,

eyes blur, hands fumble,
makes the day explicit,

the night quiet,
the outside more so

and the inside glow
with warmth, with people

if you're lucky, if
world's good to you,

won't so simply
kill you, freeze you.

ALL THE WAY

Dance a little,
don't worry.

There's all the way
till tomorrow

from today
and yesterday.

Simple directions, direction,
to follow.

KID

Smaller, no recall
of not liking one's mother

given as god was
there and forever

loving learned from her
care, bemused

distraction and
much else.

EARLY READING

Break heart, peace,
shy ways of holding
to the meager thing.

Little place in mind
for large, expansive counters
such as Hulme would also

seemingly deny yet afford
with bleak moon late
rising on cold night's field.

BESIDE HER TO LIE

He'd like the edge
of her warmth here
"beside her to lie"

in trusting comfort
no longer contests
he loves and wants her.

CIRCLES

I took the test
and I'm not depressed.

I'm inside here,
I've locked the door,

become a tentative
security system,

sensory alerts, resonant
echoes, lights, long

empty hallways. Waves
crash against the breakwater.

It's dark out there
they think until daylight

lets them off the hook
again till the phone rings,

someone passing
looks in.

BE OF GOOD CHEER

Go down obscurely,
seem to falter

as if walking into water
slowly. Be of good cheer

and go as if indifferent,
even if not.

There are those before you
they have told you.

HELP HEAVEN

Help heaven up out
of nothing before it
so deep and soft
lovely it feels to
be here at all now.

SHE IS

Far from me
thinking
her long
warmth, close-

ness, how
her face lights,
changes, how
I *miss* her,

want no
more time
with out
her.

OH

Oh like a bird
falls down

out of air,
oh like a disparate

small snowflake
melts momently.

PROVINCETOWN

Could walk on water backwards
to the very place
and all around was sand
where grandma dug, bloomers up,
with her pail, for clams.

N. TRURO LIGHT—1946

Pushing it back to
night we went

swimming in the dark
at that light

house in N. Truro
with that Bill singing,

whistling on, later stuck
his head out subway train

N.Y. window, got killed on post,
smashed, he whistled

out there in the water
Beethoven's Ninth, we

couldn't see him, only
hear him singing on.

RACHEL HAD SAID

for R. G.

Rachel had said
the persons of her life
now eighty and more
had let go themselves

into the *larger* life,
let go of it, *them*
were persons personal,
let flow so, flower,

larger, more in it,
the garden, desire,
heaven's imagination
seen in being

here among us every-
where in open
wonder about them, in
pain, in pleasure, blessed.

QUESTION

Water all around me
the front of sky ahead
sand off to the edges
light dazzle wind

way of where waves of
pleasure it can be here
am I dead or alive
in which is it.

TELL STORY

Tell story
simply
as you know
how to.

This road
has ending,
hand
in hand.

CODA

OH MAX

1.

Dumbass clunk plane "American
Airlines" (well-named) waits at gate

for hour while friend in Nevada's
burned to ash. The rabbi

won't be back till Sunday.
Business lumbers on

in cheapshit world of
fake commerce, *buy and sell,*

what today, what
tomorrow. Friend's dead—

out of it, won't be back
to pay phoney dues. The best

conman in country's
gone and you're left in

plane's metal tube squeezed out
of people's pockets, pennies

it's made of, *big bucks,*
nickles, dimes all the same.

You won't understand it's forever—
one time, just *one time*

you get to play,
go for broke, *forever,* like

old-time musicians,
Thelonious, Bud Powell, Bird's

horn with the chewed-through reed,
Jamaica Plain in the 40's

—Izzy Ort's, The Savoy. Hi Hat's
now gas station. It goes fast.

Scramble it, make an omelet
out of it, for the hell of it. Eat

these sad pieces. Say it's
paper you wrote the world on

and guy's got gun to your head—
go on, he says, *eat it* . . .

You can't take it back.
It's gone. Max's dead.

2.

What's memory's
agency—why so much
matter. Better remember

all one can forever—
never, *never* forget.
We met in Boston,

1947, he was out of jail
and just married, lived
in sort of hotel-like

room off Washington Street,
all the lights on,
a lot of them. I never

got to know her well,
Ina, but his daughter
Rachel I can think of

now, when she was 8,
stayed with us, Placitas, wanted bicycle,
big open-faced kid, loved

Max, her father, who,
in his own fragile way,
was good to her.

In and out
of time, first Boston,
New York later—then

he showed up in N.M.,
as I was leaving, 1956,
had the rent still paid

for three weeks on
"The Rose-Covered Cottage" in Ranchos
(*where sheep ambled o'er bridge*)

so we stayed,
worked the street, like they say,
lived on nothing.

Fast flashes—the women
who love him, Rena, Joyce,
Max, the *mensch,* makes

poverty almost fun,
hangs on edge, keeps traveling.
Israel—they catch him,

he told me, lifting
a bottle of scotch at the airport,
tch, tch, let him stay

(I now think) 'cause
he wants to.
Lives on kibbutz.

So back to New Mexico,
goyims' Israel sans the plan
save Max's ("Kansas City," "Terre Haute")

New Buffalo (friend told me
he yesterday saw that on bus placard
and thought, that's it! Max's place.)

People and people and people.
Buddy, Wuzza, Si
Perkoff, and Sascha,

Big John C., and Elaine,
the kids. Joel and Gil,
LeRoi, Cubby, back and back

to the curious end
where it bends away into
nowhere or Christmas he's

in the army, has come home,
and father, in old South Station,
turns him in as deserter, ashamed,

ashamed of his son. Or the man
Max then kid with his papers
met nightly at Summer Street

subway entrance and on Xmas
he gives him a dime for a tip . . .
No, old man, your son

was not wrong. "America"
just a vagueness, another place,
works for nothing, gets along . . .

3.

In air
there's nowhere
enough not
here, nothing

left to speak
to but you'll
know as plane
begins its

descent, like
they say, it
was the place
where you were,

Santa Fe
(holy fire) with
mountains
of blood.

4.

Can't leave, never could,
without more, just
one more

for the road.
Time to go makes
me stay—

Max, *be happy,*
be good, broken
brother, *my man,* useless

words
now
forever.

—for Max Finstein died circa 11:00 A.M.
driving truck (Harvey Mudd's) to California
—near Las Vegas—3/17/82.